Poems and Musings

Dona Carol Bartoli

ISBN: 978-0-9979423-7-8 (Print)
ISBN: 978-0-9979423-8-5 (eBook)

Book design by John W. Warren

Published by BrookTree Media
Takoma Park, MD

Printed in the United States of America

Cover photo by Larry Lowrimore. The Vendemmia, Villa Torquato. Montecatini Alto, 2020 (Used by permission)

Contents

Dedication

As she lay dying, my mother told me a story that I'd never heard before. She'd spent parts of summers at Wee Green, a restaurant for the farmers and working types in western Pennsylvania established by her Neapolitan grandparents Pietro and Filomena (Elizabeth) Ciampi. During prohibition, it was a speakeasy. Dona would play outside by herself, inventing games on the long driveway that led to the front door. Stones lined the pathway, and strawberries grew wild between them. She'd start at the bottom and jump from stone to stone, all the way to the top. When she fell, she'd start over. When she made it to the top—she granted herself a strawberry.

In this posthumous collection of poetry and writings, Dona leads us from poem to poem and we receive the fruit of a rich intellectual life. What you will experience in the ensuing pages is a rare gift that we did not know even existed. We knew that she wrote poems but had no idea of the output until it blossomed all around us in the days after her passing. She lived, loved, and created a world filled with beautiful things with an endless intensity. Encompassing more than sixty years of her life, these works reveal the elaborate and evolving music of her soul.

She always loved poetry—especially Emily Dickinson, Robert Frost, Rudyard Kipling, and Sylvia Plath. Poems such as "Applause," "Time," "I Have," and "Fall" pay homage to those writers. She expands her voice in later years to embrace free verse and life's harrowing moments in "The First Attempt" and "My First Taste." We encounter Dona the poet as an eighth-grader mapping out her life, a young mother working as a secretary for a Hopkins ophthalmologist, and a sage philosopher looking back at her own life at the oak desk in the Villa Torquato library.

We've titled the collection "Vita," which translates to "life" in Italian and Latin and also means "dossier" or "resume" in English. The poem "Vita," written in 1982, is one of many instances where she is doing the spade work of self-introspection in the book. These poems are also "vital" to her existence—to her trying to understand herself and her place in the universe. Life is what the book is about.

She leaves us with a call to action. "Action is the juice of life," she writes in "Solitude." It's also clear that she had intentions for her poetry in the same poem:

"They want to stand alone
To be seen and heard
By other eyes, ears, and minds."

While this stanza refers to her poems, it can also refer to those she has left behind. "Do great things," she seems to say to us. "Be seen and heard." Now she stands alone at the top of the Wee Green driveway, and this book serves as the strawberry we present to her memory.

Love,

Dean

This project was an act of love in Dona's memory made possible by Mary, Larry, Brendan, Elaine, Ian, Emma, Christina, Mary Julia, and Quinn.

Applause

Living people we profess to be,
Placed on this earth for eternity.
Molded and shaped to fit the part,
Inscribed on every human heart.

A miraculous event, this was our birth,
And as each one emerged to Earth
A special place, a definitive face,
We're given undying grace.

To fulfill that tiny role of ours,
We must build, build, build a thousand towers,
If only to tear them down again.
We must never give up, never say when.

If after plowing through twenty years,
You are now just overcoming your childish fears,
Fight twenty years with every might
To win the fight of day and night.

Don't leave a bit or part of you
Until it does what it must do.
Use every day until it's gone
Start out again like each morning sun.

If all you do is say a prayer
For some lost soul with sins to bear,

Murmur your words with the best of care,
And God will say, that's why she's there.

You are an intricate part of an earthly play.
Study your lines every day,
And when the curtain is brought slowly down,
Let the applause of the Lord resound.

October 18, 1961

Time

Time are you here? Are you there?
Only you, time, would dare
To laugh at mortals wise
And cut us to your size.

Laugh, you fleeting moment,
Leaving us twirling in your scent
Only to reach—and fall,
For you are master, after all.

You pretend we are young
And when our sweet song is sung,
You smirk at Earth, and
In an instantaneous mirth

We grow senile and quiver
For you, time, are taker and giver.
Oh, mighty time, relinquish your hold
On this flesh and mold of mine.

Please stop—or I'll hate you, time.

To Dance

If I could dance the night away
And twirl and swirl until the day,
If I could float through every night,
My life would seem so much more bright.

Yes, I am lost in a musical roar;
I am fascinated by a moving floor.
I want to dance in a swirling trance
And lose myself in this romance.

I am a different being, a reigning queen,
I am here, I am there, I am always seen.
Oh, if only I could dance my way,
And lose the night to a dancing day.

This is my utopia, my image of life—
To dance away from every strife—
Think now, care to dance with me?
If only for an eternity?

New Year's Eve, 1961

I-95

Chickahominy
Lightfoot
Toano
Tappahannock
Monongahela
Seneca
Chesapeake
Seminole
Potomac
Massaponax
Chopawamsic
Manassas
Occoquan
Patapsco
Patuxent
Indian Head Highway
No exit—

Fall

What is fall, if not to fall
Down gracefully in all.
The splendor of a leaf
Rests warmly, close to the earth's soft,
Motherly breast of dirt.
Content with just memories, and listen
As the pounding beat
Resounds with news so sweet—
That it is fall.

A season full of rust and gold,
Surrounds the world in beauty bold
And puts winter to shame—
The fall of life is a time to fall
In love with nature
And make this season best of all,
The name of which is Lady Fall.

Vita

After it rains,
I need to lie
in the hot sun
feeling fiery,
my moment
to renew,
extend,
expand, a chance to glisten
in synthesis
with the flora
at feeding time.

When

One day I wasn't;
Then I began.
Some day I won't be;
Do until then.

And then, how can it be—
The idea of no more me.

World Death

Are you asleep, wide world, are you asleep?
If so, awaken to your kingdom falling down
And listen—as it crashes to the ground,
Or watch humanity descend into a pit so deep
And you refuse to help, you stay asleep.
Can you not hear the weeping, creeping sound?
As we beg mercy in our reddened gowns.
Intoxicated world, arise and begin your reaping,
For the harvest is now dying, lying, hoping for the
    light.
Corruption rules; materialism is crowned our queen.
And you a whirling wizard, lie dormant without
    fight.
You will not yield, I sink with fading breath,
Are you asleep, wide world? It is not night.
Are you asleep, or have you met your death?

On Being Serious

An English smile, half frown, half scorn,
A solemn gesture, a laugh unborn,
"Te Deum" sung on a Monday morn.

A martyr's mind, a piercing thorn,
The absence of a joyful ring,
The presence of voice but not to sing,

To shoulder the burdens of a king,
Oblivious to the gay part of anything.
Never to brighten a summer's day.

Unable to capture a single ray,
Asleep while the spring hurries on its way.
Caring not—that it is May.

These poor, poor people devoid of mirth,
Are scattered over all the earth.
They have that fate and since their birth,
Sit peacefully by a generous hearth.

The First Attempt

We saved the pagan babies
Before recess.
A desk lunch.
Waiting sixty turns
At the water fountain.
In the dampness
Of cement floor,
A chilling start.

There was a time when
Crayons came out on the desk,
The smell of mimeograph
Sheets—caused an equal amount
of excitement and fear.

Sister Margaret punished
　　carelessness.
Anyone caught coloring over
　　the line—
Back to kindergarten.

Red Letter Days

As I think about the days
that stand out in my life, I
first remember my Communion Day,
then comes my Confirmation and
then of course, graduation.

I will never forget my first
real date or my first formal
dance, and how I anxiously
prepared for them.
Becoming president of my class,
making the Debating team, and
freshman basketball are all
days that bring back many
memories to me.

Winning second place in the
Oratorical Contest was another
day that is outstanding in
my memories.

All of these days can in
some way be called Red Letter Days,
for they all stand out in my
life, and I hope in the
years to come I will have
many more Red Letter Days.

16

I'm not sure today
And it doesn't matter
If it was a deliberate act,
    a defiance
or a simple mistake,
But once over the line bearing down
with every color—blacks and purples
Covered the page.

Bernice Sobieski
Took me to kindergarten with my paper
Held up in degradation.
Amidst the laughter
I remember
And share with you today
My first attempt
At self-portrait.

Sister

So, Prince Charming died
In your living room one evening when you
Least expected it,
And the person who survived
Was real,
With a limited expense account
And no white horse.
And you wondered if it was
Something you said
Or secretly thought
While you whistled life and
Death tunes to
Water pipes breaking and female
Noises jiggling the
Beginning of an honest
"Who you are" relationship
Against a dream—
Daydreams, night dreams,
Who's the man, struggling
On the living room floor?
Give him a real hand—
Hold on.

Ode to an Italian Poppi

Dino Bartoli, who is he?
He is husband, Dad and Poppi.
He is fixer and breaker.
He is giver—not taker.
He is a happiness maker.
He is the garden care-taker.
He is a real EARTH SHAKER.

That is Daddy to me.

Thirty-five years of hard work spent,
of scrimping and saving and paying the rent,
of working on the railroad and doing his best,
of painting and scrubbing and never a rest,
of shopping and rushing to give Mom a hand,
It's my father who is this kind of man.

He loves all his children who will never know
How hard it was to help them grow.
He polished their shoes, he listened to blues,
He sacrificed each day without pay
And none of his children remember to say—
THANK YOU, DADDY.

What kind of man devotes his life
To his grandchildren, children, and to his wife?
He is a very special man, I'll dare to say

And I'll say it loud on any day
But especially on Father's Day
TO SAY
That's your dad.

Daddy's Gone

Come when the olives and grapes are ready for
    picking.
Use your pencil and eraser.
Give all your love away—like my father.
Get old if you can.

Dino John Bartoli, Hall of Famer,
First son of Torquato and Gemma Bartoli
Conceived in the New World,
Now reunited with the love of his life,
The beautiful Caroline as she softly touches his
    hand.

He is survived by four spaghetti benders,
Emma, Mary Julia, Ian, and Quinn.
Get old, if you can.

Hate

A boiling pit of acid,
Turning wildly—
Blue skies of ugly images,
Conjure shapely demons to Leap at death.
Filthy mud and pools of blood,
Sinning into the depths of hell,
And then screams. . . .

Love

Caring, fondling someone who cares,
Picking cherries on the highest peak,
Eating the earth up to its fullest.
Running, pursued, laughing, and green hills.
Taking nature as your own—pleasure.

I Have

I've been on top.
I've been below.
I've watched love drop.
I've felt it grow.

I've held it tight.
I've loosened my grip.
I've seen its flight.
I've sailed the ship.

I've felt the pride.
I've made the grade.
I've taken the ride.
I've martyred the trade.

I've played the game.
I've won the most.
I've captured a name.
I've played the host.

I've walked in praise.
I've lived to take.
I've spent my days.
I've been a fake.

I've nothing—

The Trouble with Booze

There's too much drinking
Going on here.
That's what I said,
After another beer.

There's too much drinking,
And wasting time.
That's what I thought,
As I was sipping my wine.

There's too much losing:
Aren't we out to win?
That's what I was thinking,
When I smelled the gin.

There's too much joking about alcohol.
That's what I was feeling,
Up against the wall.
There's too much lying
About what we drink,
And that's the trouble with booze—
I think.

August 1984

My First Taste

It was winter in '63 when I took that
long ride with my father.
I shivered as he drove my prized possession
to the used car lot. I was numb—
he was embarrassed. He didn't talk—
I was glad—there was nothing left to say.
A few months before, I was celebrating my
    independence.
I saved my paychecks, proudly made my first
big financial investment, a royal-blue 1958 T-Bird.
You have to understand—it was more than a car—
it was a vehicle to freedom.
It was the first
in a series of right and wrong moves.

It had become increasingly difficult to live at home.
It was time to break the shell, and I was pushing.
With the motor racing, I drove the car to its
    100-mile-per-hour limit.
My friends screamed with excitement—later we
    toasted
with a bottle of sparkling champagne,
It was my first taste.
I was a little girl with a big toy.
I was taking chances, risking the old to find the new.
A good Catholic girl who no longer believed in
    organized religion.

I felt trapped by society, and I verbally denounced,
to anyone who would listen, the absurd structure of
    our lives.
I wanted to break away from everything all at once.
I didn't hear anything but the sound
of my own voice until I realized that I was pregnant.
You might say things came to a screeching halt.
I knew right from the beginning, even though
It was my first sexual experience.
My friends assured me it wasn't possible,
The odds were with me, they said—they were
    wrong.
Some of my girlfriends told me they had been
sleeping with their boyfriends for years.
I was surprised but not consoled.
I had never been to an all-night diner, but I needed
    one now.
There are a lot of diners in Baltimore, and I hit them
    all.
When I couldn't drink any more coffee, I decided to
    get married.
I waited three months before I walked down the
    aisle.
All my bridesmaids wore white, and so did I.
One of the first things to go was my car.
My husband was in school, and I was supporting us.
My father said he had a friend who owned
a used car lot, and maybe under the
    circumstances—

As we drove into the lot, his friend was waiting.
I sat in the car, trying not to hear what my father
    was saying.
I noticed the empty bottle of champagne on the
    back seat.
I was shivering—it would always be cold in February.

The Histrionic

Outside, many are handsome or beautiful
Inside, oft exploding, troubleful.

Thomas Young
Wrote about them in 1840,
Freud was fooled by one

Artistic and dramatic genes
Are often there

Doing it their way
Happens every day
(Frank Sinatra)

Organization is one skill
Bending others to their will

Cannot tolerate being told
What to do and not to do

Money matters are disdained
When spent, unexplained

Always needing more,
Their lives a freebie store

Self-aware of a constant voice
Bored listeners have no choice

The brains of many are quite good,
Wanting only to be understood

Front and center on their stage
Needed at any age
Try to move them,
Absorb their rage
Labored logic is not their skill
Flashes of clarity filet the core
Of both friends and foes

Whittling and belittling is their game
Chip them down to their level of pain
They are solid, confident of their world

Quick to criticize
Bristle when criticized

Periodic temper tantrums
Burn to crisp their targets.
Intense friendships burned away,
Only scattered ashes remain

Anger bursts slug the guts
Targets fight or walk
Some come back another day
Some never forgive
And forever stay away

Who will help them see the light?
How to teach them not to fight

When it is over, their sea is calm
As if it never happened.
Those left behind
Quaking, pale and exhausted

Built-up anger needs release
Once vented, leaves inner peace
Their bouts of thunder
Rent families asunder

Through their lives they learn
Who will accept them without concern.

Carefully picking with whom to fight,
Making mistakes worsens their plight
Leaving them
Solitary and lonely

The Moving Pieces

Life flows in repeating rows
And we listen to the same

I am called to see the patterns
And am aware
Of all the moving pieces
Flowing forward
In a mystical equation,
Like the constant breathing
Rhythm of the sea.

I often sense the circle
And I know
Is—is
forever universal and unchanged.

I need to know the answers
So I listen to the same
Making shapes of natural energy
When it's spilling from my brain.

July 1981

To Tell the Truth

There was Truth; I harbored it
And played a role as hypocrite.
There was a Truth; I buried it
and told reality I had quit.

Deceit is wild; it takes a shrew
To live with lies, cast out the true.
So Truth, pushed from heart and mind,
Sought shelter of another kind.

Lies, lies, she cries, are devil's ties.
Unloose yourself to me,
Bring out the savior that never dies.
Truth lives in eternity.

There was a Truth; I set it free
and now it is a part of me.
There was a Truth; there was a man,
Those two don't fit in any plan.

May 1962

The Darkest Dye

And now it's done
The deed of love
Yet who are we
To shun our destiny?

And now we end—
We stop the flow
Diverting it to channels
We will never know.

Halting emotions of the past,
Inserting words into a requiem
For now the darkest dye is cast,
One word resounds—Amen.

Yet, my love can live alone.
Say goodbye if you must, condone
The crushing of the love you've known.
My lot, to wish our love had grown.

June 1962

Preserves

I am myself tonight
        needing—
Out of myself's self tonight
        Reaching—

Myself, alone

Ah, yes, I love to say, ah, yes,
It thinks I am wise to that other
        girl
Who listened to voices of search
Who planned, worried, helped,
schemed, soothed,
        mothered,
        sistered,
brothered, loved.
Who scrambled eggs
        for thought
Who scrubbed the floors
        for feeling

Who together gathered fresh ideas
of all themselves' selves and
Shelves of canned preserves of friendship
        stored—

Labeled in jars of many names—
For the long winter is ahead,

When myself's self comes
         reaching in.

Dona and Caroline

She's a jewel
More valuable
Than a precious gem.
Her jewelry was always
Neatly tucked away
In boxes
In her dresser drawers.
When I was little, I
Spent time with her rhinestones.
I played with her pearls.
I put her dangly earrings on
And shook my head dramatically
From side to side.
She had summer jewelry and winter jewelry—
She had beads of every color.
I'd stare in her mirror
And wrap the beads around my head.
Jewelry?
She had jewelry.
She loved it.
And she hated it.
And quietly wished
That it was real.

The Answer

It was written in the clouds today
That such as I would pass your way.
The wind foretold a rendezvous,
But fate and sky were much too blue.

On the first day of this November,
I saw the Georgetown I remembered,
And with a letter in my hand,
I journeyed through a memory land.

To Kiki's first, to reminisce on
Many things I've often missed.
I walked the cobblestones again,
And someone said, "Remember when—"

A sight for painters to behold,
Were the leaves of your campus, brown and gold.
As those leaves fell slowly down,
They too met death upon your ground.

To lift them up and give them life,
Would be the answer to your strife,
But they seemed content to die their way.
So such as I went unseen today.

November 1961

Solitude

I often did not do
What I was told

Little do they know
That from each of them
I keep their special strength and wisdom

Men and women on this earth
How many ways to show their worth
Seeing strength here and weakness there
Charges life with thought and care

Each person in life, a large mosaic
No part is new, all archaic
Brain, heart, body, and soul
Small parts make up a whole

Each a tale of sizes, shapes, or colors
From ancestors, alive or dead
Known or told by family lore
Brought by sperm or egg
From their genetic store

Some see themselves as others see them (Burns)
Others have not a clue
How I think and how I do
Surprises me when each day is through

Contemplate the whys and whens
Sorting long-time goals from fleeting yens
Each day is a mixed bag
Doing for today, tomorrow, or some unknown end

Soak not in endless quandering
Belay mental wondering
Pointless pondering from ground zero
Makes no man a hero

Crystallize the problem chore
Play it in and out, aft and fore
Scope its power
Unveil its bower

Action is a juice of life
Stirring calm or calming strife
Wallow not in endless dither
Compass guide, where, and whither

Only then
From inner ken
Forge the action knives
Bold strikes of meaningful lives
See and do what has to be done
Know full well, it can be lost or won.

There are no rules
Troubled lives have no schools
Some are short and some are strong
Blessed are the short,

Endless woe from the long

By patience for when time will tell
For peace to calm the inner well
Waiting has its wisdom
In our human kingdom

I never know when
The urge to write will demand
Release and build a poem

Wrestling with a problem
Cogito ergo insomnia
Awake after midnight

Leave on or off the light
Curse the demon that robs my sleep
Deciding what thoughts to keep

Reading in the middle of the night
Sparks my poetic flame alight
From Dickinson, Yeats, and Kipling

Soak my soul with ferment of grain
Loosens synapses in my brain
Words and phrases tumble out
Seeking places in rhymes and rhythms

They cannot be forced
They bubble forth, coming alive
Demanding variety
Seeking truth and clarity

They want to stand alone
To be seen and heard
By other eyes, ears, and minds
Who welcome a kindred soul or thought
Too precious to be sold or bought

Then each identity knows it is not alone
Comfort from and for a fellow man
Who says:
This I have seen before
This I have heard before
This I have thought before

And will again, somewhere, some day
When we have gone our lonely way

Content inside
Secure with pride
Armed with knowledge of fellow men
Who showed their worth
To others, on this, our earth

Friendship

Dear Mary Carol:
A thank-you-note for a gift unexpected.
Warmth is friendship—it smells of
    Rich ingredients baking.
Reality is friendship—sincere, truth,
    Words,
Spoken, thought, read in silver wise men books
And silver tongues of youth searching for:
Freedom is friendship—a delicate veil of
Fluttering wings coloring the sky butterflying
Its way to life through:
Love is friendship—the mysterious answer
To the fear of God and heaven and Earth is:
The warmth of the reality of freedom
    Through love—or it is a
    Gift of butterflies and cakes and
        Cookies and books.

Facts, Scenarios, and Thoughts

Were the core of my brainy life
Standing on the shoulders of former men
We grow the Knowledge Tree
Thick of trunk, branches broad
Elements slowly flow
Some leaves die and fall

Religion

Dangerous—pretentious fools!
You don't understand the game.
Why are you teaching the rules?

Goodbye—ancient pied pipers—
Your holy verse, it's not the key.
Why are you walking backward?

Without your simplistic answers,
Your sacred piety—
We might have heard the question
And answered honestly—

Life and Death

It is over now, our quiet world
Bursts wildly into sound
And all the earth resounds in
Gigantic reformation.

A ripple in the sea, another move
And two instead of one swim out
The stream of life until
The waiting dirt feels sensation
On its back.
The cowering earth bends down
To tread of generation
And waits the upheaval of
Human wars and stains of
Liquid red transforms its shade
Of black to human rust.

An inch of time and still
It lays awaiting the day
When a quiet world returns
And Adams and Eves become the clay.

It is Just a Feeling—
I Know it Will Pass

Tonight, I saw a falling star.
Oh, little star, how small you are,
Higher up than all the rest,
Quickly you fell upon Earth's breast.

What prompted you, oh sailing light,
To leave the heavens with such flight?
Were you ousted from your place,
And hurled into our time and space?

What was your sin, great diadem,
That made you no longer a part of them?
What evil doing made you descend
And brought your shining to an end?

What makes our egos soar so high
And yearn to be diadems in the sky?
What makes ambition rule our souls,
And leads us to egotistical goals?
If stars can't hold their place in the sky,
How can you—how can I?
It is just a feeling
I know it will pass.

Long Shadows

Be with me, for the summer is ending—
Sending its first long shadows
Across the path we've traveled
With daring passion
In broad daylight
When sunshine's fires burned so boldly.
Soon youth's promise will be broken
    . . . and I am afraid.
I cannot climb the walls that surround you.
Must I gather only my memories
And hold them close to my heart—
Ticking
In time
With yours
Getting older
Minute by minute—
Too old for wandering?
Soon, our nights will grow longer
And colder.

Be with me . . .
At the hearth I've kept burning
In the hope of your arrival.
I long to rest
Beside you
Remembering the beauty of our fire
From the glow of our embers.

Parties

Wax burns
Drips
Spills
As it
    Hardens
Into night pictures
    Tribal images
Flashing Romeo's lament
    Eternal Juliet.

Secret melting promise
    Passing parties
    Foolish shadows
Up against the wall.

Bodies near dark time
Set fires
To hold the flaming night
Away from day.

Tired eyes—see—
    Dying candles and
Free the burning wax
    Drip
     Spill
And
  Harden.

       Summer 1981

Shining

One, two, buckle my shoe
Three, four, shut the door
    My mother's coming.
I stepped on a tack
I can't go back.
    My mother's coming.
I burned the pan
    But—I can!
    My mother's coming.
All the drawers are clean—
  I still have Dean.
    My mother's coming.
A dirty book—
    You took a look.
    My mother's coming.
A broken wrist—
    I'm sorry, Sis—
    My mother's coming.

You're here in time
  It's daughter-shine
  My mother's coming.
One, two, buckle your shoe
Three, four, open the door—
My mother's coming.

1982

The Mind

The matter of my mind
Feeds on current
Junk for thought
Piled on a collective
 Heap
Spewing smoke.
We spend time together
 When we can.
A mysterious relationship,
You yell out the answers
And I
Only hear pieces of the power
As they filter through layers
Of frozen matter.
I strain to see
 The patterns
And wait for our quiet
 Time together in the fog.

What is Summer?

Summer is the glow on pavements
A perfume for nature to fling
At all the world so that they
May drink of this new spring.

To see the glow yet not to go
And praise this three-month queen,
Is quite a crime in this our time,
Which never goes unseen.

A bath of sunlight, an ocean's roar,
A lover for a month or more
Fluttering often, alone to the shore
This is summer's season lure.

It's a broken heart, it is a lazy night,
It's an orange-red moon nearly out of sight.
Sounds as though it's a sweating Earth.
It's people who are charged with mirth.

A flood of tears behind the eye,
Afraid to live, afraid to die,
Summer is a seasonal lie,
And all its promises—amount to a sigh.

Summer of 1961

The Beauty of God

Glance at the sky, gaze at the ocean,
Survey the world around you,
The acme of loveliness in motion,
Is the hand of God.
Perceive the tranquility of His home.
Receive His glorious presence at the rail,
Never wander, child of God, never roam,
For here is beauty.
The glorious magnitude of our Catholic faith,
Is a heavenly gift from He who lived to die;
Cherish it, nourish it, guard it forever,
Never let it be defied,
For your immaculate soul of grace,
Must walk with beauty.

Eye of the Needle

South 95
Emergency Stopping Only
Dip
Right Lane
Old 25
Yield
Warning
Mormon Tabernacle
Old 18
On Ramp
To Northern Virginia
Glen Echo
Chain Bridge—Closed
Old 15
Great Falls
Wide Load
Next Right—Next Left
    Leasing
    Lodging

Barricade on Shoulder
Merge—Right
End Construction
Battlefield
Weigh Station
    Bainsville

The Place of Destination

Betty is standing at the doorstep of Caroline's Beauty Shop. Caroline is in her shop, ready, and open for business. It is Saturday morning—Caroline is only in her shop in the morning on Saturdays. Lucky for Betty she got there in time. Caroline embraced Betty with a soft touch and welcomed her as an object of beauty and strength. Caroline and Betty mingled like old friends understanding that they had spent some time living and dying in the same place. Now they have time to chat.

Caroline helped Betty into her chair, pumping her up as they chatted. Caroline pumped Betty up to the proper height, but even though she had her special shoes on, she still wasn't tall enough to work on Betty. Caroline gave Betty's hair a good brushing. She used the #2 brush with the pink handle. Betty's hair needed a good brushing. Then the discussion whether to go soft blonde or brown takes place. Soft blonde was the order of the day. The dye is cast, the color is good, and Caroline finds her favorite medium-size rollers. She hands Betty the bobby pins. "Open them and put them on your finger," Caroline says. Betty complied. They worked and chatted until her hair was set and she was ready to go under the dryer. Caroline gets Betty situated under the dryer with a hair styling magazine to read. Betty brought one of her favorite books instead. That was OK with Caroline. She knows Betty has a mind of her own. She knows that Betty keeps it real.

Betty sits under the dryer for about an hour and is soothed and relaxed by the dryer's heat. Caroline is waiting for her when she is finished. They chat again because there is no rush; they have time now. First, they discuss the style. Betty tells Caroline to do whatever she thinks. Betty leaves it up to Caroline. Caroline likes that because she is free to use all of her magical skills.

Caroline removes the rollers gently so as not to destroy the curl. She chooses a soft brush with a pink handle and teases each curl away from Betty's head. Not a stiff tease, just enough to give Betty a little "poof" around her face—clean lines, not curly—a nice wave, soft and sophisticated. Caroline takes off the towel from around Betty's shoulders. Her work is done. She sprinkles a little powder on Betty's neck and helps her put her pearl earrings back on. "La Bella Figura" is important to Caroline. Betty is not sure what that means, but she thinks it has to do with always looking her best. She knows she and Caroline will share many future appointments together. They have time to chat now.

And just in that moment, Betty hears them calling her. Caroline watches as her friend goes forward to take her place of destination.

There she goes.

Long Before

Long before I knew you, I knew you.
A soft but manly voice
Calling me from my youth to
Make a womanly choice.

Long before I kissed you, I kissed you.
Close to nature, a sky of blue,
Spring seething in hearts and minds,
A kiss of kisses—the perfect kind.

Long before I loved you, I loved you.
A tower of compassion, understanding
    Ambition.
Weak and humble—ready to listen
Waiting in the shadows for the all-
    Important cue.

December 1960

"U"

There was a time,
When everything was fine,
And then a time,
When it was great.
What happened next,
Of course, was fate.
Time took the fine,
And then the great,
And I'm left behind
The parting gate—
Waiting for the hand of fate,
Waiting here for time.

February 25,1965

Me

I'm not me
    Yesterday
There's more today
and less of me
Without tomorrow

Spring 1982

My Likes and Dislikes

Being as average teenager I enjoy
basketball, good books, dances, parties
social, and softball, but the
thing I really like most is talking.
I'm in my glory when I'm
all alone in my room with
a speech I've just written.
Debating is another thing I like
to do and even if I don't win,
it is fun just being able
to express what I feel.

I've been playing the piano
for over four years and I
wouldn't stop taking lessons for the
world. Its wonderful to be
able to sit down and play
something the way you want.
If I get into a bad mood I can
sit down and play and I can
forget who or what I was angry at.

I dislike Elvis Presley, teenagers
that smoke, indecent language,
bad movies and not being able
to go out on Saturday night.
Oh, yes I like writing autobiography
for Sister Carla Marie.

The Wind

There was a long, horizontal layer,
It was there so I stopped,
Only to rest, and then it moved and circled
The best part of life and swerved
Round and round, surrounding my
Thoughts and ideas—

And then the wind, so free it blew,
I long to succumb to its call,
But in my heart I knew my
Musicalless merry-go-round held me
Steadfast, clinging to me, so that I'd never
Be free—

And so I'll sit, only traveling the
Span of an old and worn-out road,
Too dizzy to pull my body loose
And so the circumference of life I'll be waiting
Waiting for the wind to blow softly by,
Just waiting for a glimpse of the
Wandering wind.

To Mrs. G

Where is God? He reigns above,
He abides in a kingdom created for love,
And all about Him in heavenly hazes,
Have naught to do but chant His praises.

Where is God? He reigns on Earth,
He is the spirit who inspired our birth,
And all about Him in earthly hazes,
Are not yet able to sing Christ's praises.

Where is God? He reigns within,
He abides in the soul cleansed of sin,
And all the world in daily hazes,
Practice with each breath the Almighty's praises.

Where is Michael? He is above,
He abides in God's kingdom created for love,
And all about him are heavenly hazes,
Listening—while Michael begins God's praises.

Boys in the Attic

There are little boys
in the attic
Playing with their madness
Fanatics in the attic
they are called.
Closeted.
The dust planners
design another toy
to blow our brains
into the sky.
Little pieces of what
we are scattered on their
drawing board.
Oh, Lord.
When the keeper of the dreams
is a joker,
anything can happen.
I know where the gun is
It's pointed to my head
I'll do what I'm supposed to
If you'll tell me when I'm dead.

August 1984

It Travels

I am here, and you are here,
But my soul has fled from me.
It travels forward without fear,
After one who eternally flees.

Day is night; night is day,
As onward my soul perseveres.
Searching secretly so that I may
Capture him and clasp him near.

He was in love, and I was in love,
But obstacles hindered our way.
So onward my soul, with wings of a dove,
Flies hastily to catch him, if it may.

Perhaps it will be; perhaps it will not,
It is just a matter of time,
Till my soul captures what it sought,
And forever our hearts will then twine.

1959

Pioneers

No plastic pilgrims
In this room
Real pioneers
Living
Testament in part
To regeneration.

She walked the Isthmus of Panama
Pregnant
Determined, courageous, remarkable
She made the crossing.

Daughters of the future
Have the strength
To go the distance
Renew energy
Remember her spirit
Make it.

A man/child, alone frightened
Severino, you are an illegal alien
Stranger in a strange land
Searching, you make your own way.

Daughters of the future
Reach out of disappointment
New directions

Rekindle his warmth
For others
To share.

Made in England—The Johnson Company
Is coming through him
Without enough, too many children
He does what he has to do in the
Coal mines.
It's dark, but he is a light.

Daughters of the future
Dig in to get out
Without maps
You recreate chances
Know it is OK to try

Antoinette, you are betrothed
Trunked trousseau is on board
A young girl in a new world
Defiant Italian lace
Matriarch of the family
For more than one hundred years.

Daughters of the future
Have the message
Understand destiny
Reinvest her commitment
Rebel.
Become.

My Plans For the Future

I've been thinking about what to write in this chapter but, I have not been able determine exactly what I want to become. Many times I thought my vocation was an actress but now I'm not so sure.

To go to a business school after I finish high school has always been one of my ambitions.

I'd like to become a secretary for a doctor but I'm not completely excited over the idea.

The most essential of my ambitions is to become a lawyer. I guess that must sound pretty silly because women lawyers are scarce but, if I ever think there's a slight chance I'll follow it through.

For now, I'm going to go through my four years and I'm sure I'll have all my plans for the future by the time I'm ready to make my life in this world!

71

Growing Up

The warnings gradually came,
Like whispering breezes by.
To me they were a game,
So smart was I.

Their sound grew louder to the ear.
But my world was riding high,
And my heart never held the fear,
That adulthood would pass me by.

Rather than become of age,
Let the voices continue,
I'd never surrender to a graying cage,
I'd sound my own cue.

The warnings eventually ceased,
I stayed upon my floating cloud
And now they are diseased,
And I am lost in a wandering crowd.

Old D

Time was when Old D
Said yes to everything
But I know there was a
Lot more "no" than she was
Admittin'.
Just felt guilty 'bout sayin' no—
Yes has a way of makin' folks
Feel real happy,
And that must have been
Important to Old D, back then.
She just had to leave them
Doors wide open—all the time.
"You all come in now—ya hear?
Would you like somethin' else?"
Down home hospitality.
Got to talkin' to Old D yesterday
On her back forty about them
Grits we had for breakfast
Last week in Virginia.
I said, "That sure was some
Pile of mush," and Old D
Said, "I reckon it was."

Purpose Enough

Poetry by objective
    Directives?
List principles
    Structure
        Soul?

No purpose? One purpose?
    Stipulate?
To be a
Weighted package
Filled with sand.

Future testament—
    Resisted!
A poem to consider
    Free-flowing fingers
        No gloves.

Long- and short-term
    Debris
Conceptualized barriers
    Harness
Pure possibility.

Emerging
    Itself
Generates creative sources
Purpose enough
    For existence.

September 17, 1981

Stitch in Time—Saves Nine

Stitched in time
Sewn together
In a chin-cushioned
Orbital crouch
Nine Chinese wise men
Connect—
Hem to hem.

Linked bodies
Corralled by
Center beams
Reflect a corded union—
A bodied circle.

Knotted beings
Hooked to the
Original cause
Celebrate
Universal ties
In supporting rings.

Nine Chinese wise men
One binding spirit
Fused in a braided
    Existence
Stitched in Time
    Together.

October 13, 1981

Corvette

Smashed Plastic
Spinning over-heated
Pressed to its limited
    edition
Nearing self-destruction
No shock collision
Head on
Too highly tuned—
You can't remember
Still unaware—
The degree of impact
    Needed
To become scrap.

Dear John

Stop a minute
Double double
Toil & trouble
Wishing, watching
Whirling Derby
Days of daily
Dealing, breathing,
Wheezing, wheeling,
Winning, spinning
    Top –
Stop! a minute
You're a keeper.

1982

Dona Carol Bartoli

Dona Carol Bartoli was born in Baltimore in 1942. She attended The Catholic High School of Baltimore and obtained degrees from Villa Julie College (now Stevenson University) and Morgan State University. She accomplished her lifelong dream of becoming a lawyer at the age of forty-eight, graduating from UIC John Marshall Law School in Chicago. She practiced family law in Woodstock, Illinois, for more than twenty years—opening her own practice on the Woodstock Square in 1996. She was a passionate advocate for children during custody battles. Dona and her husband of more than forty-five years, Larry Lowrimore, renovated Villa Torquato, a magnificent sixteenth-century home in Tuscany with stunning views, and their olive oil is cherished annually by friends in Italy and America. She spent her final days there. The poems and writings in this book were discovered among her papers.